SUMMER MATH WORKBOOK

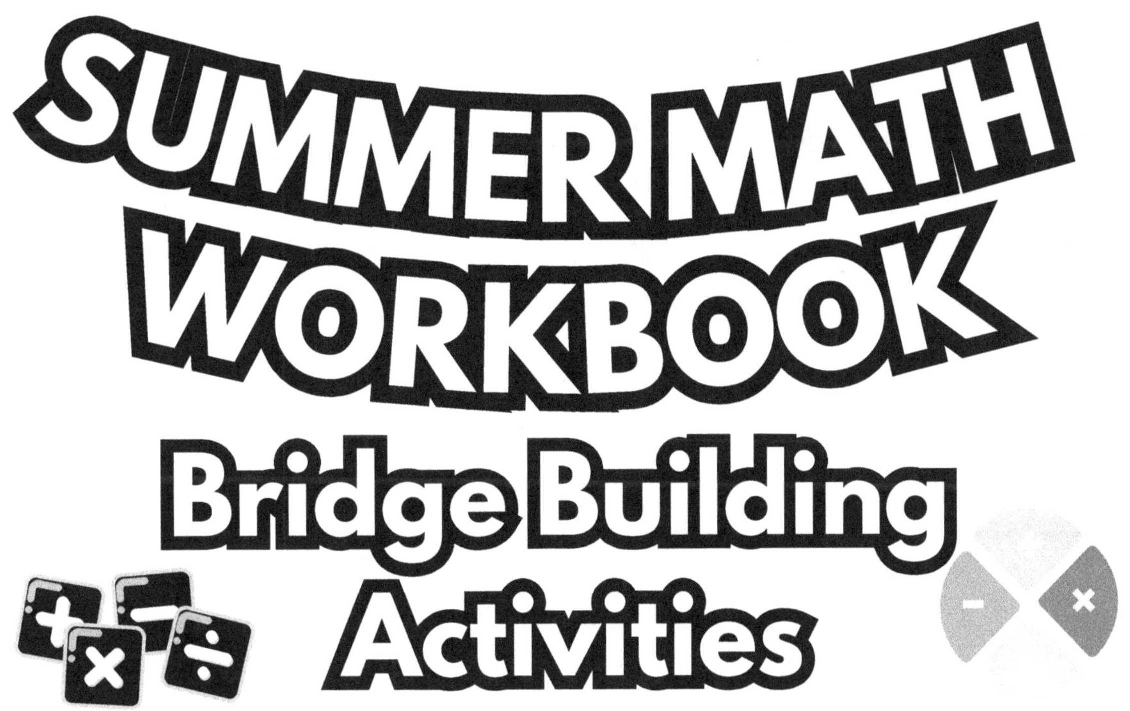

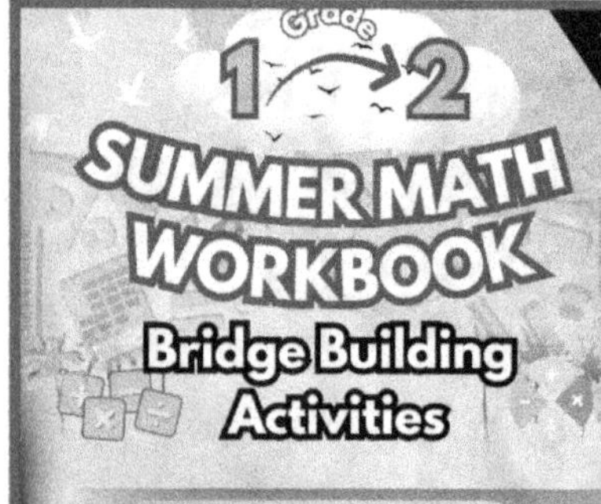

Grade
1 → 2
SUMMER MATH WORKBOOK
Bridge Building Activities
Number Sense
Addition and Subtraction
Place Value

Grade
2 → 3
SUMMER MATH WORKBOOK
Bridge Building Activities
Number Sense
Addition and Subtraction
Place Value

Grade
3 → 4
SUMMER MATH WORKBOOK
Bridge Building Activities
Number Sense
Addition and Subtraction
Place Value

Grade
4 → 5
SUMMER MATH WORKBOOK
Bridge Building Activities
Multiplication and Division
Place Value and Units
Fractions and Geometry

Grade
5 → 6
SUMMER MATH WORKBOOK
Bridge Building Activities
Multiplication and Division
Factors and Multiples
Fractions and Geometry

Grade
6 → 7
SUMMER MATH WORKBOOK
Bridge Building Activities
Arithmetic
Algebra
Geometry and Statistics

Grade
7 → 8
SUMMER MATH WORKBOOK
Bridge Building Activities
Ratio and Percentage
Algebra and Cartesian Plane
Geometry and Statistics

Grade
8 → 9
SUMMER MATH WORKBOOK
Bridge Building Activities
Ratio and Percentage
Algebra
Geometry and Graphing

Grade
9 → 10
SUMMER MATH WORKBOOK
Bridge Building Activities
Factoring and Distributing
Algebra
Geometry and Graphing

Introduction

As parents and educators, we understand the pivotal role that mathematics plays in shaping a child's academic journey and future success. Yet, the path to mathematical proficiency can often seem daunting, filled with challenges and complexities. That's where the transformative power of Summer Bridge Building Activities books comes into play, illuminating the way forward with clarity, precision, and purpose.

Summer vacation is a time for rest and relaxation, but it also presents the risk of the "summer slide," where students lose some of the academic gains they made during the school year. Summer Bridge Building Activities books are specifically designed to tackle this challenge, ensuring that your child stays academically engaged and prepared for the upcoming school year. These books provide a seamless bridge from one grade to the next, reinforcing essential skills and introducing new concepts that will give your child a head start.

Imagine your child eagerly diving into the pages of a Summer Bridge Building Activities book, greeted by clear, engaging content that demystifies complex mathematical concepts. With each turn of the pages, they embark on a journey of discovery, encountering thoughtfully curated practice questions that reinforce learning and sharpen problem-solving skills. As they unveil the answers to those questions, a sense of accomplishment blossoms within them — a tangible reward for their hard work and dedication.

Summer Bridge Building Activities books transcend traditional educational tools; they are meticulously crafted to build a deep and enduring understanding of mathematics. These books follow a sequential and logical progression, starting from fundamental principles and advancing to sophisticated problem-solving strategies. Each chapter is designed to build on the previous one, ensuring a solid and comprehensive foundation for future learning.

Parents, we yearn for nothing more than to see our children thrive academically and personally. We want to witness the spark of inspiration ignited within them as they overcome academic challenges with confidence and poise. Summer Bridge Building Activities books serve as indispensable partners in this noble endeavor, offering not just practice questions but the keys to unlocking a world of academic and personal opportunities.

Visualize the pride on your child's face as they master a challenging math concept, the joy they experience when their efforts yield results, and the confidence they gain with each success. These pages are designed to make learning math a positive, enriching, and deeply rewarding experience that will benefit them throughout their academic journey and beyond.

For educators, Summer Bridge Building Activities books are invaluable allies in the quest to cultivate mathematical proficiency in the classroom. Accompanied by comprehensive guides and readily available answers, instructors can focus on mentoring and nurturing their students, secure in the knowledge that these books provide a robust framework for effective learning.

Within the pages of Summer Bridge Building Activities books lies not just the promise of academic excellence, but the seeds of a brighter future. By integrating these resources into your child's summer routine, you are bestowing upon them the gifts of confidence, curiosity, and a lifelong love of learning.

Invest in your child's future today with Summer Bridge Building Activities books — because every great journey begins with a single step, and this step can change everything. Keep the momentum of learning alive over the summer, and watch your child soar to new academic heights.

Contents

Grade
7 - 9
PRE ALGEBRA
WORKBOOK
BRIDGE BUILDING
ACTIVITIES
Equations, Inequalities and Expressions
Linear Equations Graphing and Slope
System of Equations Quadratic Equations

Grade
6 - 8
PRE ALGEBRA
WORKBOOK
BRIDGE BUILDING
ACTIVITIES
Equations One Side and Two Sides
Verbal Algebra Expressions
Linear Equations and Slope Order of Operations

Grade
5 - 6
PRE ALGEBRA
WORKBOOK
BRIDGE BUILDING
ACTIVITIES
Integers, Mixed Numbers Decimals and Fractions
Place Value Exponents and Roots
Percentage and Ratio Word Problems

PRE ALGEBRA
WORKBOOK
for
Beginners
Integers Fractions, Mixed Numbers
Place Value Exponents and Roots
Percentage Ratio Conversion

PRE ALGEBRA
WORKBOOK
for
Adults
Integers Percent and Ratio
Equations, Inequalities Expressions
Order of Operations

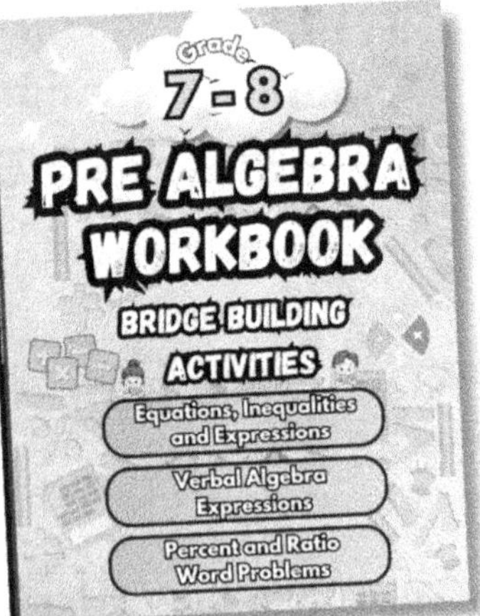

Grade
7 - 8
PRE ALGEBRA
WORKBOOK
BRIDGE BUILDING
ACTIVITIES
Equations, Inequalities and Expressions
Verbal Algebra Expressions
Percent and Ratio Word Problems

Grade
9 - 10
PRE ALGEBRA
WORKBOOK
BRIDGE BUILDING
ACTIVITIES
Equations and Inequalities Verbal Algebra
Linear and Quadratic Equations
System of Equations Polynomials

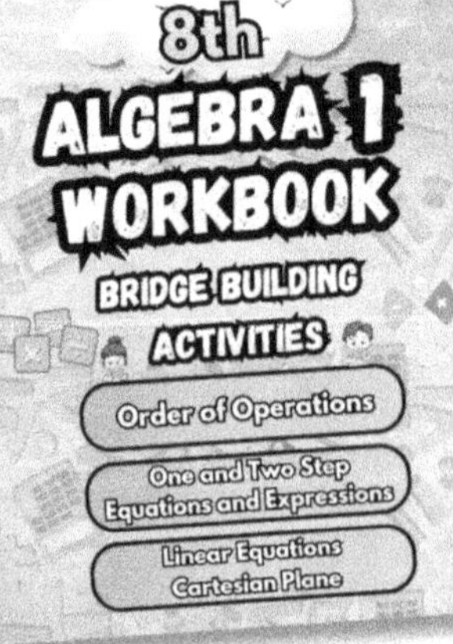

Grade
8th
ALGEBRA 1
WORKBOOK
BRIDGE BUILDING
ACTIVITIES
Order of Operations
One and Two Step Equations and Expressions
Linear Equations Cartesian Plane

Grade
7 - 9
ALGEBRA 1
WORKBOOK
BRIDGE BUILDING
ACTIVITIES
Integers Order of Operations
One and Multi Step Equations and Expressions
Linear, Quadratic Equations Equations One Side, Two Sides

Operations with Integers

Positive and negative integers are whole numbers that can represent quantities greater than zero and less than zero, respectively.

Positive Integers: Positive integers are whole numbers greater than zero. They are denoted by the numbers 1,2,3,4…

Negative Integers: Negative integers are whole numbers less than zero. They are denoted by placing a negative sign ("-") before the numbers, such as $-1,-2,-3,-4,…$

The positive integers are used to represent the number of objects, scores, etc. whereas the negative integers can be used to represent debt, losses, temperatures below freezing points, etc.

Let's solve some problems:

1. $6 - (-8) - 9$

- Start by simplifying within the parentheses:

$$- (-8) \text{ becomes } 8.$$

- Rewrite the expression with the simplified part:

$$6 + 8 - 9.$$

- Now perform addition and subtraction from left to right:

$$6 + 8 = 1\,4, \text{ then } 14 - 9 = 5$$

2. $(-5) - (-3) + 10$

$$(-5) + 3 + 10$$

$$(-5) + 3 = -2, \text{ then } -2 + 10 = 8$$

Operations with Integers

Evaluate Expressions.

1) $(-6) + (-5) - 9 =$

2) $(-4) - 7 =$

3) $3 - 10 + 3 =$

4) $2 - (-1) - 10 =$

5) $2 + (-1) =$

6) $(-9) + (-3) =$

7) $(-10) - (-7) - (-9) =$

8) $(-8) - (-8) =$

9) $9 + (-2) =$

10) $3 - 9 + (-8) =$

11) $5 + (-6) =$

12) $5 + (-9) + 6 =$

13) $1 + 1 - 9 =$

14) $(-8) - 10 + (-5) =$

15) $(-4) - (-8) =$

16) $6 - (-8) =$

17) $7 - 7 + 2 =$

18) $2 - 1 + 9 =$

19) $3 + 7 - 5 =$

20) $9 + 4 - 8 =$

21) $(-5) - (-4) =$

22) $8 - 5 + 3 =$

23) $(-10) - (-6) =$

24) $3 + (-8) - 5 =$

25) $(-4) - (-7) =$

26) $(-10) + (-10) - 4 =$

27) $(-3) + (-10) + 8 =$

28) $(-7) + 10 + (-4) =$

<u>**Order of Operations (PEMDAS)**</u>

The order of operations, often remembered by the acronym PEMDAS, stands for:

- **Parentheses**: Perform operations inside parentheses first.
- **Exponents**: Evaluate exponents (powers and roots) next.
- **Multiplication and Division**: Perform multiplication and division from left to right.
- **Addition and Subtraction:** Perform addition and subtraction from left to right.

The order of operations helps to clarify which operations should be performed first in a mathematical expression to ensure consistent and accurate results.

- **Parentheses**: Evaluate expressions within parentheses first. If there are nested parentheses, start with the innermost ones and work your way out.

  1. Example: $2 \times (3 + 4) = 2 \times 7 = 14$

- **Exponents**: Evaluate expressions with exponents (powers and roots) next.

  1. Example: $2^3 + 4 = 8 + 4 = 12$

- **Multiplication and Division**: Perform multiplication and division from left to right.

  1. Example: $2 \times 3 + 4 = 6 + 4 = 10$

  2. Example: $6 \div 2 \times 3 = 3 \times 3 = 9$

- **Addition and Subtraction**: Perform addition and subtraction from left to right.

  1. Example: $2 + 3 \times 4 = 2 + 12 = 14$

  2. Example: $10 - 4 \div 2 = 10 - 2 = 8$

Order of Operations (PEMDAS)

Evaluate Expressions.

1) $(9^2) \times (7^2) + 6 =$

2) $9 + 1 + 7 + 9 =$

3) $8 + 7^2 =$

4) $8 + 10 + 4 + 10 =$

5) $1 \times 9 \times 4 =$

6) $(10 + 2)^2 =$

7) $10 + 4 + 10 =$

8) $7(4 + 3) =$

9) $9 \times 1 \times 1 =$

10) $(10 + 4)^2 =$

11) $8 + 5 + 4 =$

12) $8 \times (7 + 7) =$

13) $(7 \times 9) - (8 + 10) =$

14) $6 \times 4 \times 9 =$

15) $(1 + 2)(2 + 6) =$

16) $7 + 4 - 9 + 5 =$

17) $(4 + 2)(9 + 7) =$

18) $5 \times 3 + 4 =$

19) $3 \times (1 + 10) =$

20) $(6 \times 10) - (4 + 10) =$

21) $(3 + 7)^2 + (7 + 3)^2 =$

22) $4 + 3 - 6 + 3 =$

23) $(2 + 5)^2 =$

24) $10 \times 2 + 7 =$

25) $2 \times 2 \times 4 =$

26) $5 + 8^2 =$

27) $1 + 10^2 + 4 + 4^2 =$

28) $(5 + 1) \div 3 =$

<u>**Solving Equations (One Side)**</u>

Solving one-step equations involves performing a single operation to isolate the variable and find its value.

Let's solve an equation step by step: $16 + x = 31$

1. **Identify the Goal**:

   The goal is to isolate the variable x on one side of the equation.

2. **Simplify the Equation**: Combine like terms on both sides of the equation, if necessary.

   The equation is already simplified.

3. **Undo Addition or Subtraction**: If there's addition or subtraction involving the variable, undo it by performing the opposite operation on both sides of the equation.

   Since x is being added to 16, we'll undo this operation by subtracting 16 from both sides of the equation:
   $$16 + x - 16 = 31 - 16$$

4. **Isolate the Variable**: Ensure that the variable is alone on one side of the equation.

   $$X = 15$$

5. **Check Your Solution**: Substitute the value of x back into the original equation to verify that it satisfies the equation.

   $$16 + 15 = 31$$

   $$31 = 31$$

The equation is balanced, so the solution.

Equations (One Side)

Solve for the variable.

1) $6z - 1 = 53$

2) $38 - 4y = 2$

3) $4 \div m = 1$

4) $5 + 3x = 32$

5) $1z + 6 = 10$

6) $k + 10 = 16$

7) $x + 2 = 6$

8) $5 \times k = 35$

9) $y \times 1 = 1$

10) $12 - 9z = 3$

11) $3z + 10 = 34$

12) $5 + k = 8$

13) $64 \div y = 8$

14) $8x - 8 = 40$

15) $9 + 7m = 44$

16) $x \times 7 = 7$

17) $k \times 1 = 3$

18) $1 \times k = 6$

19) $x \times 5 = 25$

20) $27 \div x = 3$

21) $7x - 6 = 29$

22) $x \times 3 = 9$

23) $7 + x = 13$

24) $18 \div x = 3$

25) $30 \div x = 5$

26) $y - 7 = 2$

27) $9x - 5 = 85$

28) $2y + 6 = 10$

29) $10k - 7 = 73$

30) $8 \times m = 56$

Equations (Two Sides)

A two-sided equation is an equation where both sides have expressions with variables and constants. The goal when solving a two-sided equation is to find the value of the variable that makes both sides equal.

For example: Let's solve an equation:

$$9 + 8x + 8 = 64 + x + 2$$

- Combine Like Terms: Simplify each side of the equation by combining like terms (terms with the same variable or constants).

$$9 + 8x + 8 = 64 + x + 2$$
$$17 + 8x = 66 + x$$

- Isolate the Variable: Use inverse operations to isolate the variable on one side of the equation.

$$\text{subtract } x \text{ from both sides:}$$
$$17 + 8x - x = 66 + x - x$$
$$17 + 7x = 66$$
$$\text{subtracting 17 from both sides:}$$
$$17 - 17 + 7x = 66 - 17$$
$$7x = 49$$
$$\text{divide both sides by 7:}$$
$$\frac{7x}{7} = \frac{49}{7} = x = 7$$

- Check Solution: Once you find the solution, substitute it back into the original equation to ensure it makes the equation true.

$$\text{Substitute } x = 7 \text{ back into the original equation:}$$
$$9 + 8(7) + 8 = 64 + 7 + 2$$
$$9 + 56 + 8 = 64 + 7 + 2$$
$$73 = 73$$

Equations (Two Sides)

Solve for the variable.

1) $9 + 4z = 12 + z$

2) $9 + m = 2m$

3) $3y = 36 - y$

4) $48 - x = 5x$

5) $2z = 5 + z$

6) $4y = 24 + y$

7) $27 - x = 2x$

8) $26 + y = 4 + 6y + 2$

9) $2y = 9 - y$

10) $2m = 6 - m$

11) $7 + m = 8m$

12) $26 - z = 7z + 2$

13) $1 + k = 2k$

14) $4 + 4k + 6 = 19 + k$

15) $4 + 8z + 8 = 16 - z + 5$

16) $5z = 18 - z$

17) $2k + 12 = 4k + 8$

18) $31 - k + 11 = 5 + 5k + 1$

19) $37 + m + -5 = 2 + 4m + 9$

20) $6 + 2x + 3 = 21 + x + {-3}$

21) $1 + 2z + 5 = 8 + z$

22) $50 - 2x = 3x + 5$

23) $24 - y = 5y$

24) $3k = 32 - k$

25) $7m + 4 = 108 - 6m$

26) $66 - 6m = 1 + 7m$

27) $5 + 7y + 8 = 69 - y$

28) $34 - 5k = 6 + 9k$

<u>**Solving One-Step Equations**</u>

Solving one-step equations involves finding the value of the variable that makes the equation true. In a one-step equation, there is only one operation (addition, subtraction, multiplication, or division) performed on the variable.

The goal is to isolate the variable on one side of the equation by performing inverse operations.

<u>**For example:**</u>

Given the equation $6 = -3z$, where we want to solve for z.

The given equation is already in the form of a one-step equation, with z being multiplied by -3.

To isolate z, we need to perform the inverse operation of multiplication, which is division.

Divide both sides by -3:

$$\frac{6}{-3} = \frac{-3z}{-3}$$

Simplify:

$$-2 = z$$

So, the solution to the equation is $z = -2$.

When we substitute the value of $z = -2$ back into the original equation, $6 = -3(-2)$, it simplifies to $6 = 6$. This confirms that our solution is correct because it satisfies the original equation.

Solving One-Step Equations

Solve for the variable.

1) $1 + (s \div 10) = 1.4$

2) $8 + (s \div 10) = 8.8$

3) $4 = 4 \times (z - 9)$

4) $19 = (2 \times s) + 9$

5) $16 = z \times 2 + 4$

6) $4 = 4 \times b$

7) $80 = 7 \times k + k$

8) $16 = 1 + (5 \times a)$

9) $1.1 = 1 + (s \div 9)$

10) $32 = s \times 8$

11) $49 = 4 + (9 \times z)$

12) $3 \times k + k = 8$

13) $21 = 4z - 3$

14) $14 = 8 + (6 \times z)$

15) $30 = 4 \times k + k$

16) $31 = 6x + 7$

17) $y \times 2 - 9 = -7$

18) $z + (8 \div z) = 6$

19) $1 + 10b = 81$

20) $30 = a \times 5 + 10$

Solving Two-Step Equations

Solving two-step equations involves finding the value of the variable that makes the equation true. In a two-step equation, two operations (addition, subtraction, multiplication, or division) are performed on the variable.

The goal is to isolate the variable on one side of the equation by performing inverse operations in the reverse order of operations.

For example:

Given the equation $18 = (10 + b) - 2$, where we want to solve for b.

To solve for b, we need to undo the operations that have been performed on b.

1. Undo the subtraction by adding 2 to both sides:

$$18 + 2 = (10 + b) - 2 + 2$$
$$20 = 10 + b$$

2. Undo the addition by subtracting 10 from both sides:

$$20 - 10 = 10 + b - 10$$
$$10 = b$$

So, the solution to the equation is $b = 10$

Let's substitute $b = 10$ back into the original equation to verify if it satisfies the equation:

Original equation:

$$18 = (10 + b) - 2:$$

Substitute $b = 10$:

$$18 = (10 + 10) - 2$$

simplify:

$$18 = 20 - 2$$
$$18 = 18$$

Since the equation simplifies to 18 =1 8, it confirms that our solution $b = 10$ is correct.

Solving Two-Step Equations

Solve for the variable.

1) $26 = 4x + 10$

2) $3s + 8s + 2s = 78$

3) $28 = 9z + 5z$

4) $4k - 4 + 8k = 80$

5) $24 = m^2 + m - 6$

6) $60 = (7 + y) \times 6$

7) $56 = 6 + (6b + 8)$

8) $2 + (7k + 6) = 29$

9) $33 = 3 \times (7 + x)$

10) $153 = a(8 + a)$

11) $43 = 7 \times m + 8$

12) $-10 = 2 - (3 \times a)$

13) $7a - 8 + 5a = 88$

14) $12 = 2 \times (5 + a)$

15) $75 = (10 + s) \times 5$

16) $46 = 5k - 6 + 8k$

17) $10 \times (6 - y) = 30$

18) $49 = m^2 + m - 7$

19) $46 = m + 6 + 4m$

20) $2 - (10 \times s) = -18$

<u>**Evaluating Equations**</u>

Evaluating expressions involves substituting given values for variables in an expression and then performing the indicated operations to find the result.

For example: Let's evaluate $4x - 10$, when $x = 3$:

Step 1: Substitute the given value for the variable:

Replace every occurrence of x in the expression $4x - 10$ with the given value, which is 3:

$$= 4(3) - 10$$

Step 2: Perform the operations:

Perform the indicated operations according to the order of operations (PEMDAS - Parentheses, Exponents, Multiplication and Division, Addition and Subtraction):

$$= 4 \times 3 - 10$$

Step 3: Simplify:

Calculate the result:

$$12 - 10 = 2$$

Summer Algebra Workbook

Building Activities

Evaluate Equations

Evaluate each expression when: $y = 5$

1) $7y + 9 \times (y + 3) =$

2) $(7y + 5) \times (y + 1) =$

3) $1(y + 3) + y(7 - y) =$

4) $9y + y =$

5) $9y - 2 + 4y =$

6) $(7y + 3) \times (y + 8) =$

7) $2 + (y \div 5) =$

8) $(3 - y) \times 1 =$

9) $2 + y =$

10) $(3y + 6)(2y + 3) =$

Evaluate Equations

Evaluate each expression when: $y = 4$

1) $y \times (6 - y) =$

2) $2(7 + y) =$

3) $7 + 10y - (7 + y) =$

4) $4 \times y =$

5) $(y \times 5) + y =$

6) $3 \times y - 1 =$

7) $(4y)^2 =$

8) $5y + 2 \times (y + 1) - 5 =$

9) $3(y + 6) + (2y - 5) =$

10) $y + 2 + 5y =$

Evaluate Equations

Evaluate each expression when: $y = 1$

1) $8y + 3 \times (y + 2) =$

2) $10y - 8 =$

3) $y \times 7 + 2 =$

4) $(6y + 10)(2y + 10) =$

5) $2y + y =$

6) $9y + 7 =$

7) $7(1 + y) =$

8) $9 + 4y =$

9) $10 + y(6 - y) + 5y =$

10) $3 + y =$

Evaluate Equations

Evaluate each expression when: $y = 1$

1) $3(8 - y) =$

2) $10y + 10 \times (y + 5) - 5 =$

3) $y \times 10 =$

4) $y \times 1 + y =$

5) $10 + 3y - (4 + y) =$

6) $(9 + y)(9y - 6) =$

7) $(2y + 5) \times (y - 10) =$

8) $(y \div 1) + y =$

9) $y + 6 + 10y =$

10) $y(7 + y) =$

Evaluate Equations

Evaluate each expression when: $y = 6$

1) $7y - y =$

2) $5 \times y + y =$

3) $(7y + 10) + (7y - 7) =$

4) $7y + 7 =$

5) $(3y)^2 =$

6) $8y + 7y =$

7) $7 + 10y =$

8) $1 + y(9 - y) + y =$

9) $5 + (7y - y)(5 + y) =$

10) $y \times (9 - y) =$

Evaluate Equations

Evaluate each expression when: $y = 3$

1) $(5y + 7) + (8y + 3) =$

2) $8 \times y + 2 =$

3) $(8 - y) \times (y + 9) =$

4) $5(y + 10) + (7y - 10) =$

5) $5 + (8y - y)(1 + y) =$

6) $10 + 7y - y(5 + y) =$

7) $6 + y - y(5 + y) =$

8) $(5y + 9) + (4y + 7) =$

9) $8(2 - y) =$

10) $10y + 10y + 7y =$

Verbal Algebra Expressions

Verbal algebra involves translating word problems or verbal statements into algebraic expressions or equations.

For example: The product of the two numbers is 91. One number is six less than the other. What are the numbers?

We're given a verbal description of a problem, and we need to represent it using algebraic symbols and equations.

Let's break down the given problem into algebraic expressions:

- Given that the product of the two numbers is 91, we can write the equation: $xy = 91$
- Also, given that one number is six less than the other, we can write another equation: $x = y - 6$

Now, we can use algebraic techniques to solve the system of equations to find the values of x and y, which represent the two numbers.

$$x\,(x - 6) = 91$$

1. Solve the equation:

   - Expand the equation:

   $$x^2 - 6x = 91$$

   - Rearrange the equation into standard quadratic form:

   $$x^2 - 6x - 91 = 0$$

   - Factor the quadratic equation:

   $$(x - 13)\,(x + 7) = 0$$

2. Find the solutions for x:

   - From the factored form, we have two possible values for x:

$$x = 13 \text{ or } x = -7$$

3. Check the validity of the solutions:

   - Since one number is six less than the other, we discard the negative solution.

   - Therefore, the solution is $x = 13$.

4. Find the other number:

   - Substitute $x = 13$ into the expression for the other number:

   Other number $= x - 6 = 13 - 6 = 7$

So, the two numbers are 13 and 7.

Verbal Algebra Expressions

1) Four more than ten times a number is 104. What is the number?

2) The product of ten and some number is equal to the sum of that number and 81. What is the number?

3) Find two consecutive odd integers such that six times the larger decreased by the smaller is 27.

4) One-half of a number increased by 3 is 8. What is the number?

5) Five times the sum of a number and three times the number is 60. Find the number.

6) 4 is equal to the product of two and some number. Find the number.

7) Six times a number is 0. What is the number?

8) A number diminished by 4 is 7. Find the number.

9) The quotient of a number and ten increased by 7 is 10. What is the number?

10) Ten times the difference of 6 minus a number is 20. What is the number?

11) The quotient of a number and eight increased by 5 is 12. What is the number?

12) The difference of two numbers is 38. The larger number is 6 more than five times the smaller number. What are the numbers?

13) The product of eight and a number is 48. What is the number?

14) The sum of two numbers is 8. One number is two less than the other. Find the numbers.

15) When a number is divided by two, the result is 5. What is the number?

16) The sum of three consecutive numbers is 15. What are the numbers?

17) One of two numbers is three more than the other. The sum of the numbers is 5. Find the numbers.

18) A number increased by nine is 15. Find the number.

19) Eight more than five times a number is equal to the number increased by 52. What is the number?

20) The sum of two numbers is 18. The larger number is two times the smaller number. What are the numbers?

21) Two more than a number is 4. What is the number?

22) The greater of two numbers is 8 less than ten times the smaller number. Their sum is 47. Find the numbers.

23) One-half of a number decreased by 1 is 1. Find the number.

24) The product of five and some number is equal to the sum of that number and 12. What is the number?

25) One of two numbers is two-fifths of the other number. The sum of the numbers is 7. Find the numbers.

26) The sum of the first and third of three consecutive numbers is 6. Find the numbers.

27) The quotient of a number and six is 7. Find the number.

28) The sum of the largest and three times the smallest of three consecutive numbers is equal to 34. Find the numbers.

29) One number is six times another. Their sum is 63. Find the numbers.

30) One of two numbers is ten more than the other. The sum of the numbers is 16. Find the numbers.

<u>Solving Inequalities</u>

Inequalities are mathematical expressions that compare the relative sizes of two values. They are used to express relationships where one quantity is:

- "$<$" (less than),
- "$>$" (greater than),
- "$<=$" (less than or equal to),
- "$>=$" (greater than or equal to),
- and "$\neq$" (not equal to) another quantity.

For example:

$$y + \text{-}10 \leq -8$$

To isolate y, we need to get rid of the constant term -10. Since -10 is being subtracted from y, we can undo this operation by adding 10 to both sides of the inequality:

$$y - 10 + 10 \leq -8 + 10$$

$$y \leq 2$$

To check the solution:

$$2 - 10 \leq -8$$

$$-8 = -8$$

The inequality is true when $y = 2$

Solving Inequalities

1)
$$\frac{z}{-7} \leq 3$$

2)
$$-5 \geq 1z$$

3)
$$-1 + y \leq -4$$

4)
$$x - 5 < 7$$

5) $21k \geq -18$

6) $-8 \leq -3 + m$

7) $\dfrac{k}{-7} \leq 2$

8) $4 \leq -9 - m$

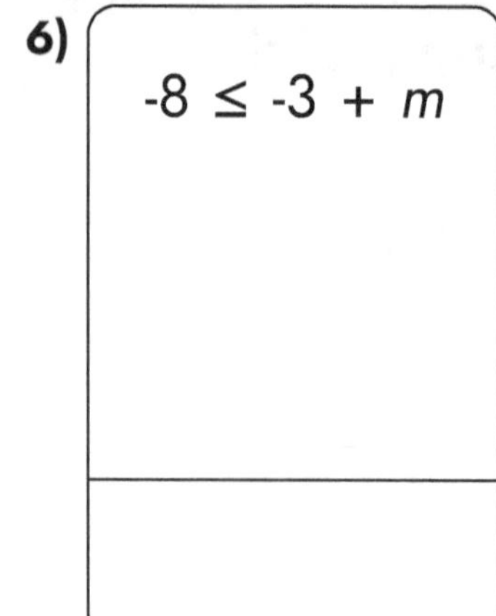

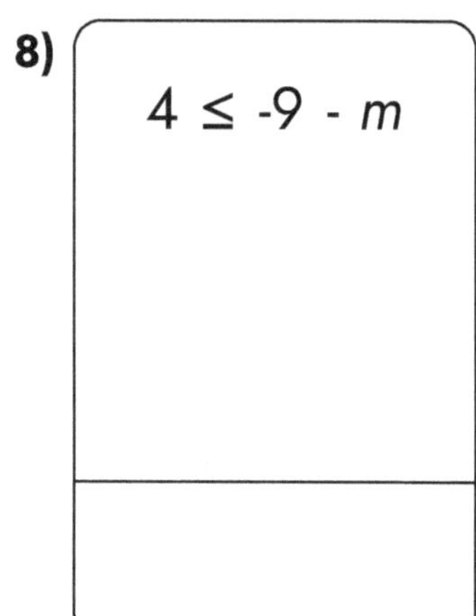

9) $-5 - m \geq 2$

10) 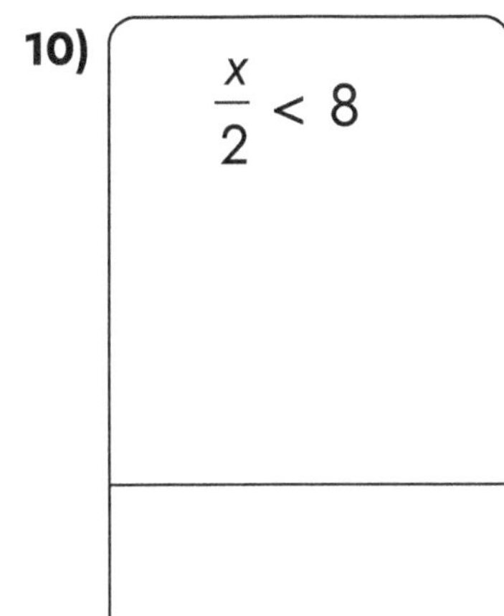 $\dfrac{x}{2} < 8$

11) $-4 \leq y + -4$

12) $-24\,k \geq -12$

13)

$$\frac{y}{7} < 2$$

14)

$$x - 2 \leq 3$$

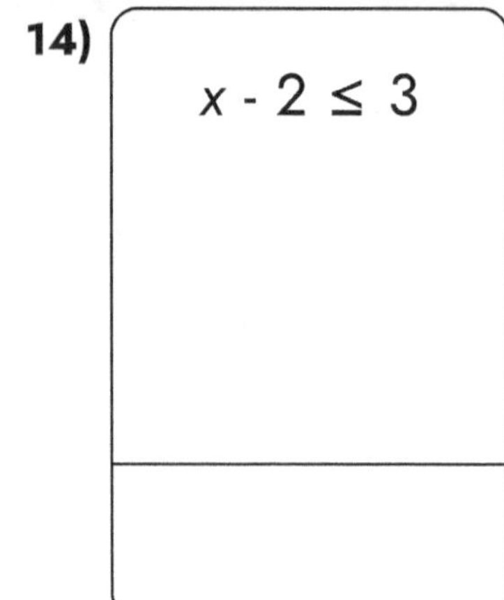

15)

$$-7 \leq 3 + x$$

16)

$$3z < -15$$

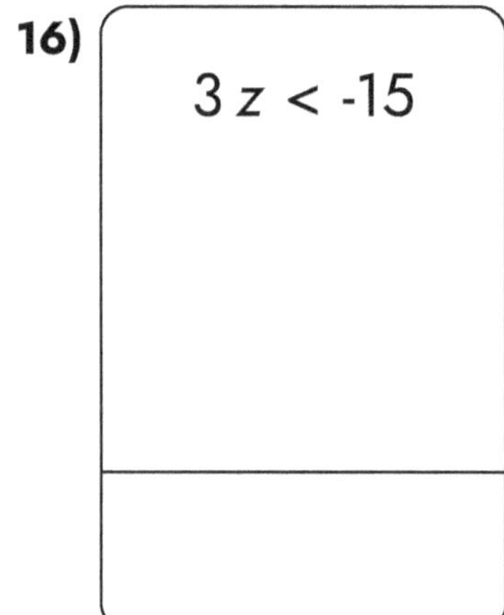

17)

$$12 < 10z$$

18)

$$y - {-7} \geq 8$$

19)

$$4 < 2 + z$$

20)

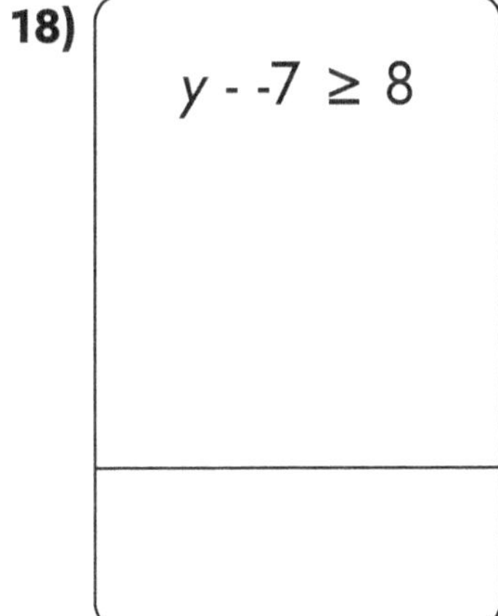

$$4 < \frac{k}{1}$$

21)

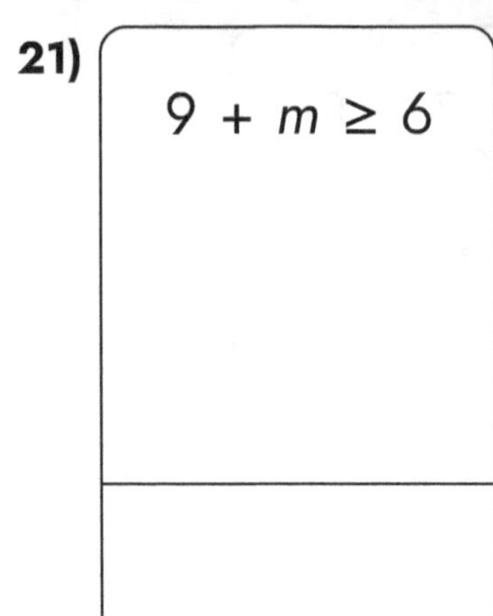

$$9 + m \geq 6$$

22)

$$m - 5 \leq 6$$

23)

$$2x < -6$$

24)

$$-7 \geq \frac{x}{-5}$$

25)

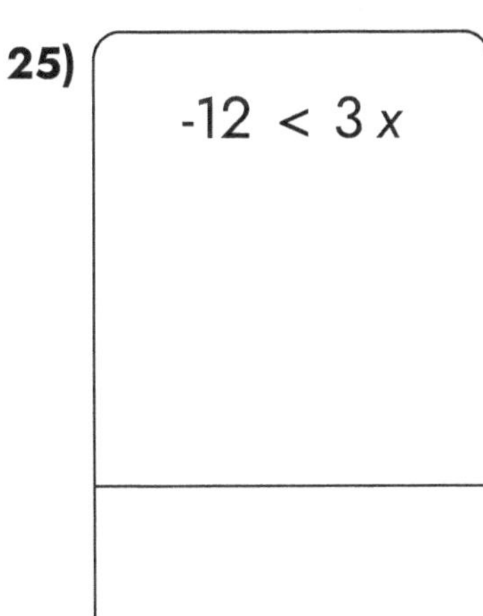

$$-12 < 3x$$

26)

$$-3 \geq y - {-5}$$

27)

$$-9 \leq 6 + x$$

28)

$$-4 < \frac{y}{-8}$$

<u>**Simplifying Expressions**</u>

It involves combining like terms and performing operations to make the expression easier to understand and work with.

Let's simplify the expression:

$$2x - 2x + 8 + 4$$

- **Combine like terms: First, we look for terms with the same variable and exponent. In this expression, $2x$ and $-2x$ are like terms, so they can be combined:**

$$2x - 2x = 0$$

- **Substitute the simplified terms: After combining the like terms, the expression becomes:**

$$0 + 8 + 4$$

- **Combine the remaining terms: Now, we add the constants together:**

$$8 + 4 = 12$$

Simplify Expressions

1) $13 - 7x + 15 - 15x + 3 - 13x$

2) $4 + 9z - 14 + 6z - 10 + 10z$

3) $10k + 13 - 7 - 4k + 6k$

4) $-4 + 18m - 7m - 14 - 8m$

5) $-18x - 9 + 7 - 14x$

6) $3x - 20 - 3x + 8$

7) $x - 16x$

8) $m + 10 + 6m$

9) $3x - 17 - 4x + 15$

10) $-13m - 20 - 10m$

11) $14x - 9 + 20x - 16 + 14x + 19$

12) $-2k - 5 - k$

13) $16 + 3k - 11 + 14k$

14) $10 + 7x - 5x + 13 - 12x$

15) $4 + k - 18 + 15k$

16) $-17x + 10x + 13 - 6x$

17) $20k + 18 - 20k + 10 + 5k + 1$

18) $8m + 2m$

19) $19x - 17 - 10x + 11$

20) $1 - 9(-7y + 6)$

21) $6y - 15y + 18y - 3 + 11$

22) $-13 + 2z - 17z - 9 - 12z$

23) $-15 + 19k + 6 - 6k$

24) $8 + 2k - 9k + 20 - 8k$

25) $x + 14x$

26) $3 + 7z - 7z$

27) $15k - k$

28) $x - 20x + 8x + 1 + 9$

29) $15z + 18 + 19z + 12 + 19z + 7$

30) $-18k + 7 + 14k$

31) $x - 9x + 6x + 16 + 2$

32) $6y - 18y + 6 + 4$

33) $13m + 20m$

34) $-k - 6k$

35) $16k - 9 - 6k + 12$

36) $-8x - 12 + 11 - 5x$

37) $10 - 3z + 10 - 13z + 10 - 10z$

38) $7x - 9 - 19x + 1$

39) $19m - 19 - 20m + 10$

40) $15k - 3k$

41) $-17k + k$

42) $15y - y$

43) $-4x - 9x$

44) $k - 16k$

45) $7 - 20(17k - 11)$

46) $12 - 4y + 9 - 13y + 14 - 3y$

47) $17k - 16 - 7k + 15 - 7$

48) $3m - m$

Graphing Linear Equation

Graphing a linear equation involves plotting the points that satisfy the equation on a coordinate plane and connecting them to form a straight line. Linear equations are equations of the form $y = mx + b$, where m represents the slope of the line, and b represents the y-intercept, the point where the line intersects the y-axis.

To graph a linear equation:

1. Identify the slope (m) and y-intercept (b) from the equation.

2. Plot the y-intercept $(0,b)$) as a point on the y-axis.

3. Use the slope to find additional points on the line. The slope represents the change in y for every unit change in x.

4. Connect the points to form a straight line.

For example, to graph the equation:

$$y = \frac{9}{4}x - 8$$

1. Identify the slope and y-intercept: The slope is $\frac{9}{4}$, and the y-intercept is −8.

2. Plot the y-intercept: Plot the point $(0,-8)$.

3. Use the slope to plot additional points: the slop is $\frac{9}{4}$ to find another point. we will move up 9 units and 4 units to the right from the y-intercept to find another point.

4. Draw the line: Once we have at least two points, we can draw a straight line.

We can continue this process to plot more points and extend the line further if needed.

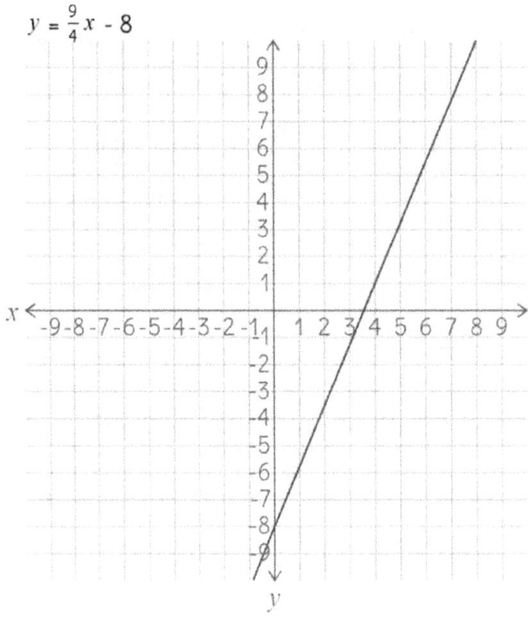

Graphing Linear Equations

1) 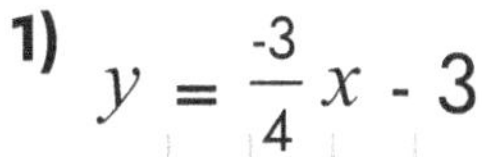
$$y = \frac{-3}{4}x - 3$$

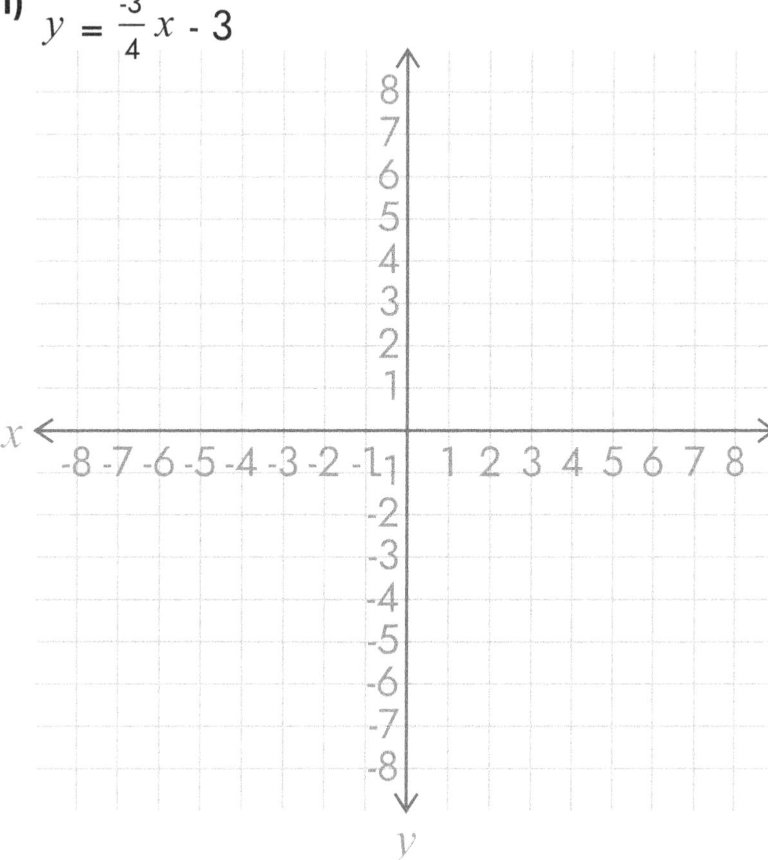

2) $y = \dfrac{-7}{4}x - 1$

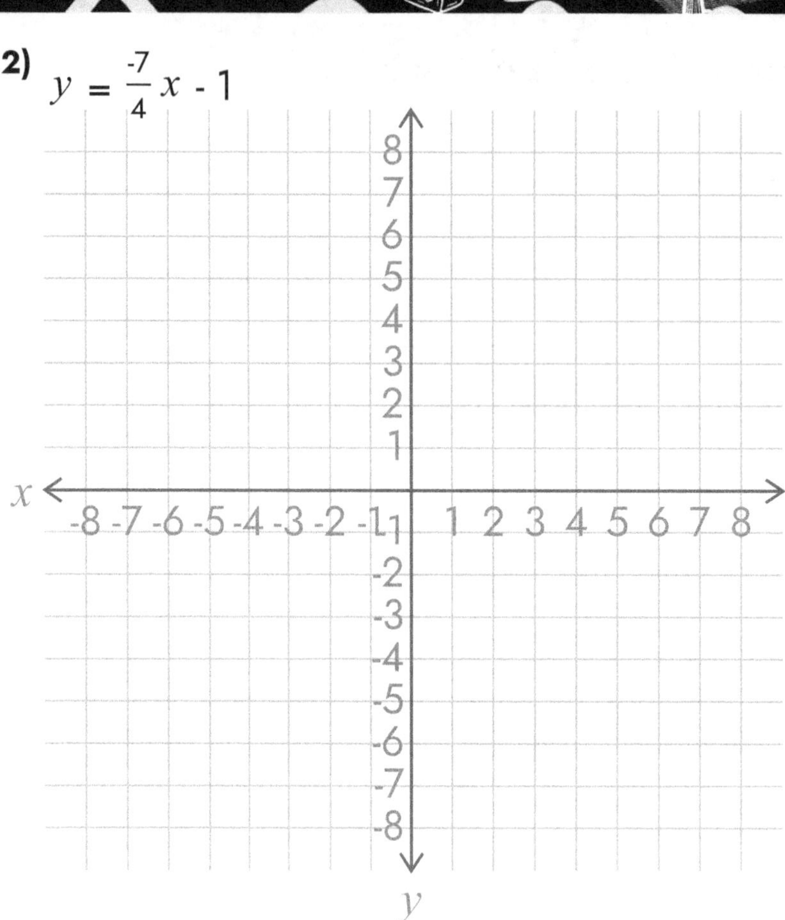

3) $y = \dfrac{11}{4}x - 3$

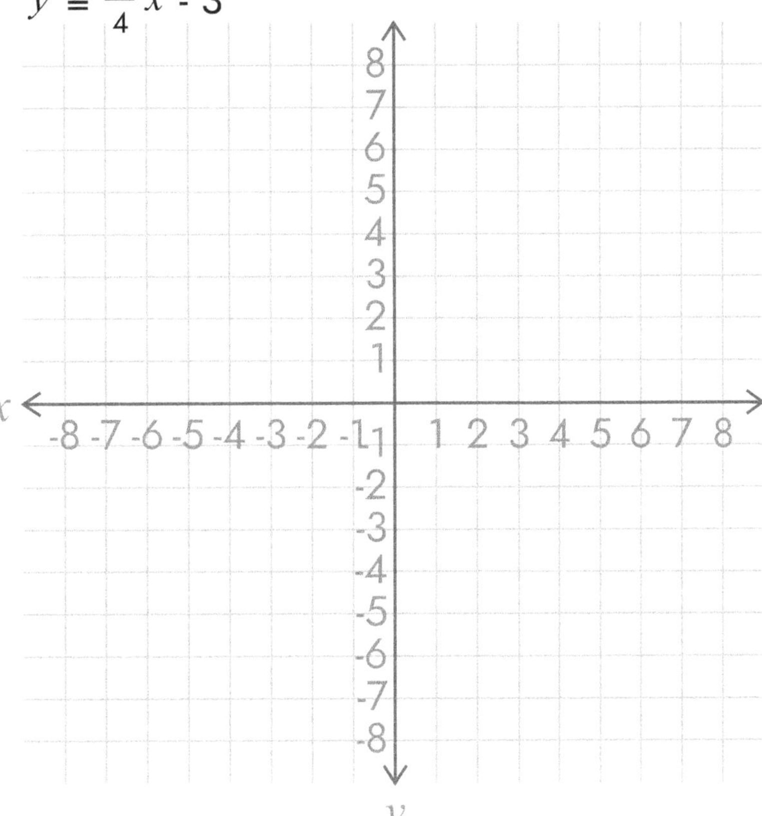

4) $y = \dfrac{1}{2}x + 4$

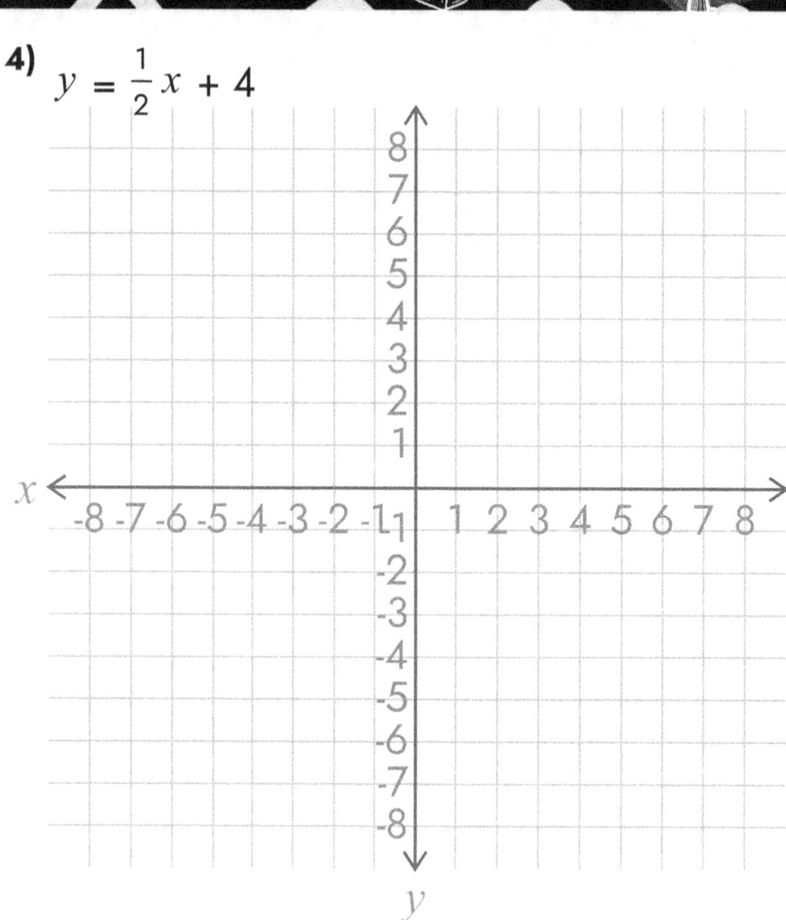

NAME: _______________

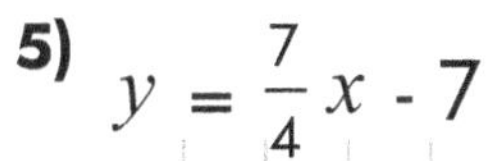

5) $y = \dfrac{7}{4}x - 7$

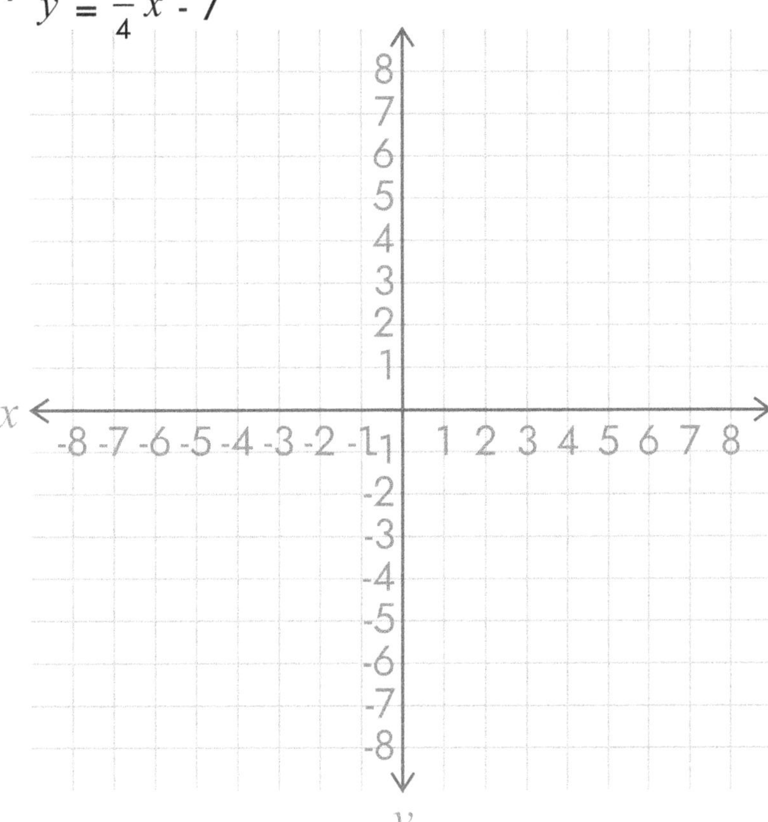

ANSWERS

Page 1:   Operations with Integers

1. -20   **2.** -11   **3.** -4   **4.** -7   **5.** 1   **6.** -12   **7.** 6   **8.** 0   **9.** 7

10. -14   **11.** -1   **12.** 2   **13.** -7   **14.** -23   **15.** 4   **16.** 14   **17.** 2   **18.** 10

19. 5   **20.** 5   **21.** -1   **22.** 6   **23.** -4   **24.** -10   **25.** 3   **26.** -24   **27.** -5

28. -1

Page 4:   Order of Operations (PEMDAS)

1. 3,975   **2.** 26   **3.** 57   **4.** 32   **5.** 36   **6.** 144   **7.** 24   **8.** 49

9. 9   **10.** 196   **11.** 17   **12.** 112   **13.** 45   **14.** 216   **15.** 24   **16.** 7

17. 96   **18.** 19   **19.** 33   **20.** 46   **21.** 200   **22.** 4   **23.** 49   **24.** 27

25. 16   **26.** 69   **27.** 121   **28.** 2

Page 7:   Equations (One Side)

1. $z = 9$ **2.** $y = 9$ **3.** $m = 4$ **4.** $x = 9$ **5.** $z = 4$ **6.** $k = 6$

7. $x = 4$ **8.** $k = 7$ **9.** $y = 1$ **10.** $z = 1$ **11.** $z = 8$ **12.** $k = 3$

13. $y = 8$ **14.** $x = 6$ **15.** $m = 5$ **16.** $x = 1$ **17.** $k = 3$ **18.** $k = 6$

19. $x = 5$ **20.** $x = 9$ **21.** $x = 5$ **22.** $x = 3$ **23.** $x = 6$ **24.** $x = 6$

25. $x = 6$ **26.** $y = 9$ **27.** $x = 10$ **28.** $y = 2$ **29.** $k = 8$ **30.** $m = 7$

Page 10:   Equations (Two Sides)

1. $z = 1$ **2.** $m = 9$ **3.** $y = 9$ **4.** $x = 8$ **5.** $z = 5$ **6.** $y = 8$ **7.** $x = 9$

8. $y = 4$ **9.** $y = 3$ **10.** $m = 2$ **11.** $m = 1$ **12.** $z = 3$ **13.** $k = 1$ **14.** $k = 3$

15. $z = 1$ **16.** $z = 3$ **17.** $k = 2$ **18.** $k = 6$ **19.** $m = 7$ **20.** $x = 9$ **21.** $z = 2$

22. $x = 9$ **23.** $y = 4$ **24.** $k = 8$ **25.** $m = 8$ **26.** $m = 5$ **27.** $y = 7$ **28.** $k = 2$

Page 16: Solving One-Step Equations

1. 4	**2.** 8	**3.** 10	**4.** 5	**5.** 6	**6.** 1	**7.** 10
8. 3	**9.** 1	**10.** 4	**11.** 5	**12.** 2	**13.** 6	**14.** 1
15. 6	**16.** 4	**17.** 1	**18.** 4 or 2	**19.** 8	**20.** 4	

Page 21: Solving Two-Step Equations

1. 4	**2.** 6	**3.** 2	**4.** 7	**5.** 5 or -6	**6.** 3
7. 7	**8.** 3	**9.** 4	**10.** 9 or -17	**11.** 5	**12.** 4
13. 8	**14.** 1	**15.** 5	**16.** 4	**17.** 3	**18.** 7 or -8
19. 8	**20.** 2				

Page 26: Evaluate Equations

1. 107	**2.** 240	**3.** 18	**4.** 50	**5.** 63	**6.** 494	**7.** 3	**8.** -2
9. 7	**10.** 273						

Page 27: Evaluate Equations

1. 8	**2.** 22	**3.** 36	**4.** 16	**5.** 24	**6.** 11	**7.** 256	**8.** 25	**9.** 33
10. 26								

Page 28: Evaluate Equations

1. 17	**2.** 2	**3.** 9	**4.** 192	**5.** 3	**6.** 16	**7.** 14	**8.** 13	**9.** 20
10. 4								

Page 29: Evaluate Equations

1. 21	**2.** 65	**3.** 10	**4.** 2	**5.** 8	**6.** 30	**7.** -63	**8.** 2	**9.** 17	**10.** 8

Page 30: Evaluate Equations

1. 36	**2.** 36	**3.** 87	**4.** 49	**5.** 324	**6.** 90	**7.** 67	**8.** 25	**9.** 401
10. 18								

Page 31:   Evaluate Equations

1. 49   **2.** 26   **3.** 60   **4.** 76   **5.** 89   **6.** 7   **7.** -15   **8.** 43   **9.** -8   **10.** 81

Page 32:   Verbal Algebra Expressions

1. 10   **2.** 9   **3.** 3, 5   **4.** 10   **5.** 3   **6.** 2

7. 0   **8.** 11   **9.** 30   **10.** 4   **11.** 56   **12.** 8, 46

13. 6   **14.** 5, 3   **15.** 10   **16.** 4, 5, 6   **17.** 1, 4   **18.** 6

19. 11   **20.** 6, 12   **21.** 2   **22.** 42, 5   **23.** 4   **24.** 3

25. 5, 2   **26.** 2, 3, 4   **27.** 42   **28.** 8, 9, 10   **29.** 9, 54   **30.** 3, 13

Page 39:   Solving Inequalities

1. $z \geq -21$ **2.** $z \leq -5$ **3.** $y \leq -3$ **4.** $x < 12$ **5.** $k \geq -6/7$ **6.** $m \geq -5$

7. $k \geq -14$ **8.** $m \leq -13$ **9.** $m \leq -7$ **10.** $x < 16$ **11.** $y \geq 0$ **12.** $k \leq 1/2$

13. $y < 14$ **14.** $x \leq 5$ **15.** $x \geq -10$ **16.** $z < -5$ **17.** $z > 6/5$ **18.** $y \geq 1$

19. $z > 2$ **20.** $k > 4$ **21.** $m \geq -3$ **22.** $m \leq 11$ **23.** $x < -3$ **24.** $x \geq 35$

25. $x > -4$ **26.** $y \leq -8$ **27.** $x \geq -15$ **28.** $y < 32$

Page 46:   Simplify Expressions

1. $-35x + 31$ **2.** $25z - 20$ **3.** $12k + 6$ **4.** $3m - 18$

5. $-32x - 2$ **6.** -12   **7.** $-15x$ **8.** $7m + 10$

9. $-x - 2$ **10.** $-23m - 20$ **11.** $48x - 6$ **12.** $-3k - 5$

13. $17k + 5$ **14.** $-10x + 23$ **15.** $16k - 14$ **16.** $-13x + 13$

17. $5k + 29$ **18.** $10m$ **19.** $9x - 6$ **20.** $63y - 53$

21. $9y + 8$ **22.** $-27z - 22$ **23.** $13k - 9$ **24.** $-15k + 28$

25. $15x$ **26.** 3   **27.** $14k$ **28.** $-11x + 10$

29. 53z + 37	**30.** −4k + 7	**31.** −2x + 18	**32.** −12y + 10
33. 33m	**34.** −7k	**35.** 10k + 3	**36.** −13x − 1
37. −26z + 30	**38.** −12x − 8	**39.** −m − 9	**40.** 12k
41. −16k	**42.** 14y	**43.** −13x	**44.** −15k
45. −340k + 227	**46.** −20y + 35	**47.** 10k − 8	**48.** 2m

Page 52: Graphing Linear Equations

1. $y = \frac{3}{4}x \cdot 3$

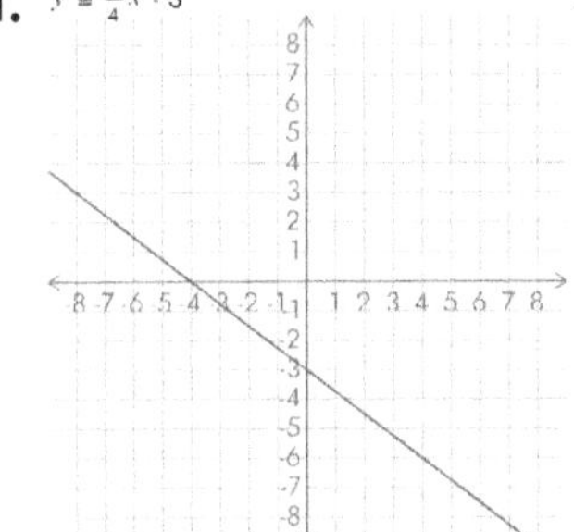

2. $y = \frac{-7}{4}x \cdot 1$

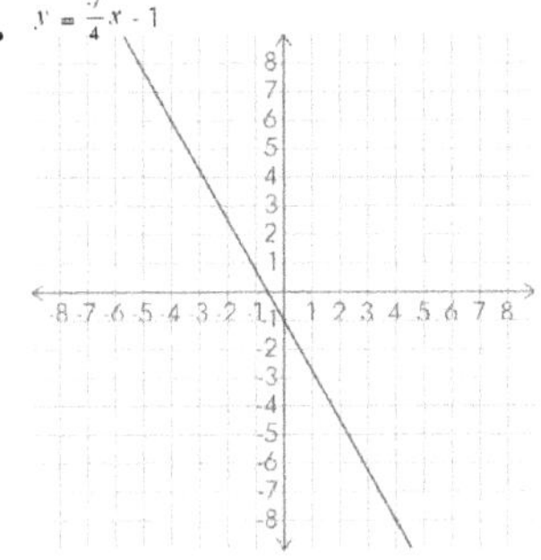

3. $y = \frac{11}{4}x \cdot 3$

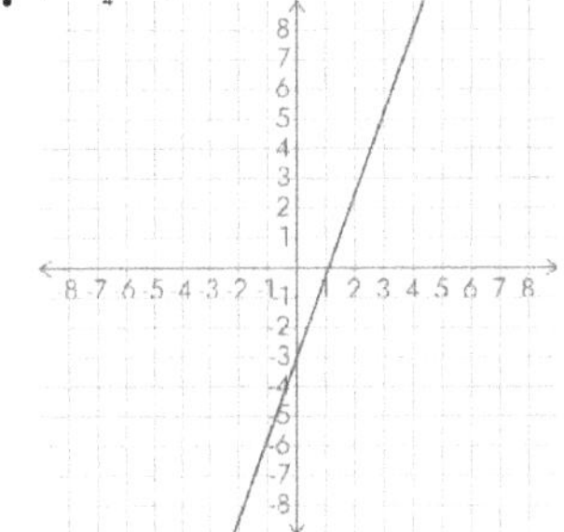

4. $y = \frac{1}{2}x + 4$

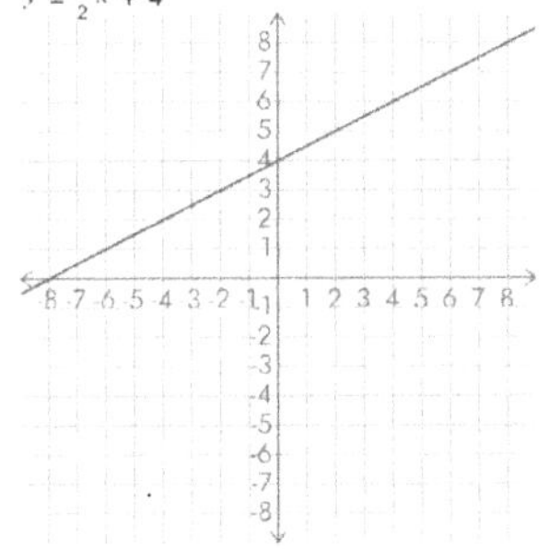

5. $y = \frac{7}{4}x \cdot 7$

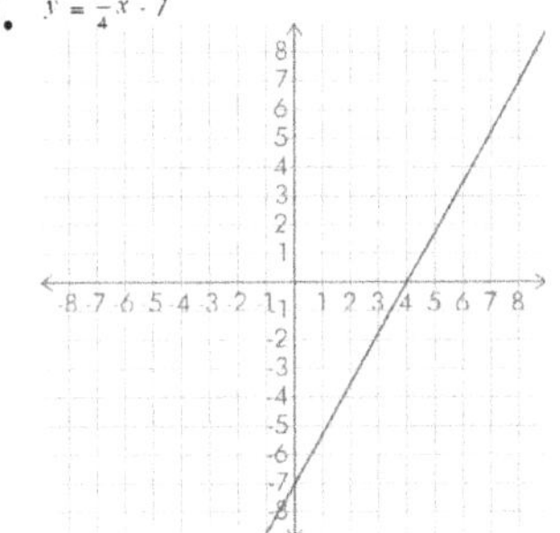